CHRISTIAN HEALING

By the same author:

The Hot Line
Doing What Comes Supernaturally
Signs and Blunders

CHRISTIAN HEALING

PETER H. LAWRENCE

Terra Nova Publications Ltd
Bristol

Unless otherwise indicated, biblical quotations are taken from the
New International Version
© 1973, 1978, 1984 by the International Bible Society.
Used by permission.

British Library Cataloguing in Publication Data.
A catalogue record for this book is available
from the British Library.

ISBN 0 9522688 7 6

Typeset by Ex Libris Press, Bradford-on-Avon, Wiltshire
Printed and bound in Great Britain by
Cromwell Press, Broughton Gifford, Wiltshire
Published in Great Britain by Terra Nova Publications Ltd.
Registered Office: 21 St.Thomas Street, Bristol BS1 6JS, England.

Contents

Acknowledgments

Many thanks to Melanie and Sally for their speedy and sacrificial typing. Thanks also to Phil and Gill who did clever things with my computer and read the manuscript. And thanks to my family – Carol, Amanda, Heather and Hazel, who allowed me to write during the school holidays instead of doing housework or homework.

Peter H. Lawrence
April 1997

ONE

The Prayer Model

Most Christians pray for the sick to be healed. Virtually every church, whatever size, denomination or culture, regularly asks God through Jesus to send His Holy Spirit in healing power on their friends and relatives who are unwell. This is an almost universal Christian declaration that God loves to heal and the healing ministry of Jesus continues today. It is a practice supported by Scripture.

'...pray for each other so that you may be healed' (James 5:16).

'...I pray that you may enjoy good health and that all may go well with you...' (3John 2).

'And pray in the Spirit on all occasions with all kinds of prayers and requests. With this in mind, be alert and always keep on praying for all the saints' (Ephesians 6:18; see also Phil.4:6;1Tim.2:1).

This is good and right and biblical.

The prayer model looks something like this –

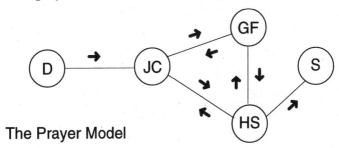

The Prayer Model

The Disciple prays to 'God the Father through Jesus Christ asking Him to send His Holy Spirit on the Sick person to heal them. There are times when this is most powerful and effective and brings glory to God.

Cynthia was over 80% disabled and for some time had been deteriorating physically. She had a chronic degenerative spinal condition with neurological disorders and functional impairment. The whole of the motor system of her body did not work properly. She saw double through very narrow tunnel vision, but at times even this was lost through muscle spasms. Cynthia had little use of her limbs and needed a specially stabilised electric wheelchair. There was no known cure for her illness and the doctors said all they could do was to make her as comfortable as possible and give her all the support they could. One doctor gave her only two years to live 'at the outside'.

Many Christians prayed constantly for Cynthia, without any evidence of physical improvement, until one night she was left on her own in the house. The family saw she was alright and went out at about 7.40 pm. At 8.30 pm Cynthia prayed, 'Oh Lord, forgive my weakness of faith. I believe, help my unbelief.' Suddenly the presence of Christ began to fill the room most powerfully. With head bent, Cynthia was aware of a glow which grew stronger and caused a tremendous brightness. Expecting to see a great light shining through the window, she looked up, but saw instead a vision of Jesus who himself was the source of this light. The overwhelming feeling was one of extreme cleanness.

Jesus very gently touched Cynthia's head and the glow spread throughout her body, giving the sensation of padlocks and chains being sprung loose. Instantly, her sight was

10

restored and her hands, feet, legs and body were straightened and could now be moved without pain. Gradually, the vision of Jesus faded and Cynthia spring-cleaned the house from top to bottom, ready for when her family returned. They were obviously overjoyed when they did, and a little fearful it would not last, but they need not have worried. Several years later she is still fit and active.

Cynthia's healing caused the authorities a few problems: at the time she was receiving a mobility allowance and now had to be investigated and examined by doctors. The verdict was to withdraw her mobility allowance because there was 'a relevant change of circumstances'. Authorities have a quaint way with words, but it is encouraging to know that simple prayer can bring about such a change.[1] I have known Cynthia for several years and it has always been a great thrill to see her clambering over seats as a member of a ministry team to pray for others in need.

In 1989 I met a man who was raised from the dead over forty years ago. Edmund came to preach in our church and stayed overnight in the vicarage. He still has his death certificate which was issued at the time. He told me how he left his body, saw the silver cord being cut (Eccles. 12:6), and had the amazing experience of talking with Jesus in heaven. Suddenly the voice of his landlady broke into the peace and joy of heaven. 'Don't let him die. Lord, don't let him die,' she prayed.

Jesus told him he would have to go back, turned him round and gave him a gentle push. Edmund returned to his body some three hours after he died, and needed to minister to the mortician when he came round. His landlady was praying these words at the time he was restored - not in the mortuary, nor even in the hospital, but some distance away at his digs.[2]

Simple prayer may lead to a direct intervention by God, bringing wholeness and healing. In our experience, prayer also works well with or through the medical profession. In December 1993 Sue was diagnosed as having a rare liver disease and from then on her friends prayed continually for her to be healed. Sue pinpoints five significant times of prayer:-

1. Peter anointed me with oil (James 5:14).

2. John Wimber prayed for me at a healing conference.

3. I received personal prayer at the Toronto Airport Christian Fellowship.

4. Attended an Easter Day service at St. Andrew's Chorleywood.

5. Prayer at the 'Lakeside' weekend conference.

Sue's faith in Christ was greatly strengthened at these times as she, her husband and four children united in love for one another and for God. They fought bravely and spent much time in prayer – but – Sue's physical condition continued to deteriorate.

Death had to be faced squarely amidst feelings of helplessness, hopelessness, anger, grief and self-pity. This struggle eventually led to peace, contentment, a quiet joy and appreciation of the simple things of life as Sue surrendered to God, telling Him to do whatever He wanted. The only human hope of physical healing was now a liver transplant.

In 1996 our church prayed and waited and it was not an easy prayer. Someone else would have to die for Sue to live. On September 29th, Sue was taken to hospital feeling very poorly with a suspected infection. We were told that if a transplant became available while she had an infection it would not be possible to have the operation. We prayed earnestly for Sue at the Sunday services.

That night I hardly slept. Taking the funerals of mothers who leave families behind is one of the hardest crosses a minister has to bear. Every moment I was awake I prayed for Sue. I know others were doing the same.

In the morning I visited the hospital. I had not seen Sue for a few weeks and was quite shocked. Her complexion was mellow yellow and her stomach the size of a woman in labour. I prayed with her for healing, and left.

Within a few hours Sue was home. In less than 24 hours news of a 'perfectly matched' donor was received. On October 2nd the transplant took place under the supervision of a Christian consultant. There were many complications, and others on the wards died following similar surgery, but Sue came through. When she walked into the Lantern Church thin, fit and rosy-cheeked the place erupted in praise for God.

I realise this story may throw up all kinds of theological difficulties for some. We could certainly use some help from Christian writers who seem to fight shy of the transplant subject – but – we are delighted to have Sue back among us and so is her family. I think God is too.

Sometimes when we pray, God intervenes directly and people are healed. Sometimes when we pray, God intervenes indirectly and people are healed. I believe prayer for the sick is a good thing and I believe it should be going on day and night in all our churches. The prayer model is very biblical and to be encouraged. It is one in which we ask the God and Father of our Lord Jesus Christ to heal.

Notes

1. This account appears also in Peter H. Lawrence *The Hot Line* (reprinted by Terra Nova Publications Ltd: Bristol 1997) p189.
2. This account appears also in Peter H. Lawrence *Doing What Comes Supernaturally*, (reprinted by Terra Nova Publications Ltd: Bristol 1997) p53.

TWO

The Healing Model of Jesus

The prayer model for healing is a good and a biblical one. Interestingly, though, there is no New Testament evidence of Jesus using it. He spent much time in prayer but none of the gospel writers records Jesus asking his Father to heal anyone. Jesus himself commands sickness to go and it goes (e.g. Mk.7:34).

Traditionally the Christian Church has argued:- 'Jesus could heal the sick because he was God.' This is a very comfortable doctrine. After I have said my prayers I can go and play golf. There is nothing more I can do.

But the evidence of the New Testament does not let me off the hook so lightly and my golf is not what it might be. While scripture does not record Jesus asking the Father to heal, neither does it say Jesus healed because he was God. We need to look at the evidence before deciding if the example of Jesus can help us to see more people healed today.

He Laid Aside His Majesty

'In the beginning was the Word, and the Word was with God, and the Word was God. He was with God in the beginning.... The Word became flesh and made his dwelling among us' (Jn.1:1,2,14).

John unfolds the mystery of the incarnation. God becomes

man.

'Though he was rich, yet for your sakes he became poor' (2Cor.8:9).

'Christ Jesus: who being in very nature God, did not consider equality with God something to be grasped, but made himself nothing, taking the very nature of a servant' (Phil.2:5-7).

It is very important in understanding New Testament healing to grapple with the idea of Jesus becoming flesh. As early as the writing of John's letters, people were saying Jesus had not really come in the flesh (1John 4:2,3). Rather like the appearance of an angel who looks like a human being – a kind of hologram Jesus. But the New Testament opposes this view (1John 1:1) and the Early Church decreed it to be heresy.

Jesus becoming flesh remains as a foundation block of Christianity from New Testament times to today and this is important in understanding the Jesus model of healing. We can deduce a number of things about Jesus' humanity from scripture. When Jesus became a man he did not lay aside his holiness or his righteousness (2Cor.5:21, Heb. 4:15, 1Pe.2:22), but it seems right to suggest that he did lay aside his omnipresence, his omnipotence and his omniscience. He was born in a stable, probably could not change his own nappy, and maybe could not speak 400 different languages while he was in the manger. Otherwise what does it mean to become flesh? There is evidence to support this as a biblical view.

'...Jesus grew in wisdom and stature...' (Lk.2:52).

Omnipresent?   – 'He is not here' (Lk.24:6).

Omnipotent?   – 'By myself I can do nothing' (Jn.5:30).

Omniscient?   – 'No-one knows about that day or hour, not even the angels in heaven, nor the Son, but only the Father' (Mt.24:36).

Jesus' Baptism

But if Jesus was neither omniscient nor omnipotent during the time he ministered here on earth in the flesh, how then did he heal the sick? The turning-point appears to be his baptism. Before then there is no evidence to suggest that Jesus ever healed anyone. In fact, when he returned to Nazareth they were completely taken by surprise and did not believe in him.

'Coming to his home town, he began teaching the people in their synagogue, and they were amazed. "Where did this man get this wisdom and these miraculous powers?" they asked. "Isn't his mother's name Mary, and aren't his brothers James, Joseph, Simon and Judas? Aren't all his sisters with us? Where then did this man get all these things?" And they took offence at him. But Jesus said to them, "Only in his home town and in his own house is a prophet without honour." And he did not do many miracles there because of their lack of faith'

(Matt.13:54-58).

The people of Nazareth were taken by surprise when Jesus began healing the sick. And – where was Joseph? 'Isn't his mother's name Mary, and aren't his brothers James, Joseph, Simon and Judas? Aren't all his sisters with us?' Only Dad is missing. He was there when Jesus was twelve (Lk.2:42) but he is never mentioned as being alive after that. His mother and brothers come to Jesus to take him home (Mk.3:20,21,31-

17

35), but Joseph is not mentioned. Surely this would be the role of a father/male guardian? On the cross, Jesus asks John to look after his mother (Jn.19:26,27) which John does. Where is Joseph? It seems logical to conclude he is dead; one person Jesus did not heal. Humanly speaking, Jesus may have even delayed the start of his ministry because of the death of Joseph, until his family was old enough to look after Mary. And here is a further mind-boggling idea. Luke records this:

'Jesus said to them, "Surely you will quote this proverb to me: 'Physician, heal yourself!' Do here in your home town what we have heard that you did in Capernaum"'(Lk.4:23).

Could it possibly be that Jesus himself needed healing? 'Physician, heal yourself!' Did he perhaps suffer from colds and flu or worse as a boy, like normal human beings? Isaiah prophesied these words:

'He grew up before him like a tender shoot, and like a root out of dry ground. He had no beauty or majesty to attract us to him, nothing in his appearance that we should desire him. He was despised and rejected by men, a man of sorrows, and familiar with suffering' (Is.53:2,3).

'A root out of dry ground' is a sick plant. When the human Jesus was pierced he certainly bled and died like the rest of us. There is no evidence of Jesus healing anyone before his baptism and some suggestions that he did not.

What Jesus did not do before his baptism will always be debatable because it is largely an argument from silence, but what follows next is very much clearer. At his baptism Jesus hears the voice of his heavenly Father and is filled with the Holy Spirit. Hearing the Father and being filled with the Holy Spirit are the two ingredients which seem to be the key to

18

Jesus' ministry. Luke records these words at its commencement.

'Jesus, full of the Holy Spirit, returned from the Jordan and was led by the Spirit...' (Lk.4:1). 'Jesus returned to Galilee in the power of the Spirit...' (4:14).

He then goes to the synagogue at Nazareth where he reads from Isaiah.

"The Spirit of the Lord is on me, because he has anointed me to preach good news to the poor. He has sent me to proclaim freedom for the prisoners and recovery of sight for the blind, to release the oppressed, to proclaim the year of the Lord's favour." Then he rolled up the scroll, gave it back to the attendant and sat down. The eyes of everyone in the synagogue were fastened on him, and he began by saying to them, "Today this scripture is fulfilled in your hearing" (Lk.4:18-21).

At his baptism Jesus hears from the Father and is filled with the Holy Spirit. At the start of his ministry Jesus links his healing ministry to being anointed by God with the Holy Spirit. Even after this, the power to heal does not appear to be permanently present. Luke 5:17 says, '...the power of the Lord was present for him (Jesus) to heal the sick.' Perhaps there were times when the power was not present and Jesus could not do any healing. When the power was present, however, it was associated with the work and power of the Holy Spirit. '...I drive out demons by the Spirit of God...' (Mt.12:28). The power to heal appears to come from the Holy Spirit. The authority to heal seems to come from God the Father.

In John 5 Jesus goes to the hospital to do some visiting. In those days it was called, 'The pool at Bethesda.'

'Here a great number of disabled people used to lie – the blind, the lame, the paralysed' (Jn.5:3). This is a particularly interesting account because it records the healing of 'one who was there' (5:5). Unlike some of the healings described elsewhere in the gospels, where 'many' (Mk.1:34) or even 'all' (Mt.4:24) are healed, this story suggests only one is healed.

The man in question 'had been an invalid for thirty-eight years.' Why then did Jesus choose to heal this one?

Question: Was he a good man?
Answer: No. Jesus said to him, 'See, you are well again. Stop sinning or something worse may happen to you' (Jn.5:14), and in the story he comes across as something of a moaner and groaner.
Question: Was he a man with a lot of faith in Jesus?
Answer: No. When asked who healed him he does not know. John writes, 'The man who was healed had no idea who it was...' (Jn.5:13).
Question: So why then does Jesus heal this one when there are many others who are blind, lame and paralysed?
Answer: Jesus gave them this answer: 'I tell you the truth, the Son can do nothing by himself, he can do only what he sees his Father doing, because whatever the Father does the Son also does' (Jn.5:19).

Jesus could only do what he saw his Father doing. So whenever the Father said, 'I'm doing that one,' Jesus did that one and the sick person was healed. The teaching implies Jesus could not heal those the Father was not doing.

Scripture would seem to suggest that Jesus came to the Father who sent the Holy Spirit to him with authority and

20

power to heal certain sick people. When the Father was doing it – Jesus did it. On Good Friday the Father was not doing healing and three men died who wanted to live. But whenever the Father was doing it He told the Son through prayer, gave him the power and Jesus did it. I picture the way Jesus healed the sick like this:

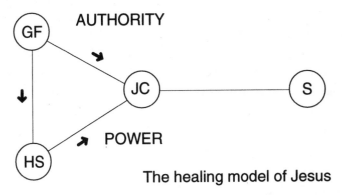

The healing model of Jesus

Whenever Jesus received the authority of God the Father and the power of the Holy Spirit he invaded Satan's kingdom and healed the sick. He did this with discernment and love - treated everyone differently - cast demons out of some yet not out of others - but commanded healing rather than asked for it.

In John 11:41,42, Jesus prays to the Father before the tomb of Lazarus.

'Father, I thank you that you have heard me. I knew that you always hear me, but I said this for the benefit of the people standing here, that they may believe that you sent me.'

Notice it is a thanksgiving prayer not a petitionary one but it seems to contain the secret of how to raise a four day old corpse. The Father is doing it, so Jesus is doing it.

'Father I thank you that you have heard me,' suggests Jesus has already prayed to the Father who has already said, 'yes'. In 11:4 Jesus knows Lazarus will be healed. In verse 5 John writes, 'Jesus loved Martha and her sister and Lazarus. Yet when he heard that Lazarus was sick, he stayed where he was two more days.'

In verse 14 Jesus says, 'Lazarus is dead....' Supernatural knowledge appears to be running right through this story, culminating in supernatural power when Jesus exercises his faith in his Father's word. When the Father says it, Jesus hears it, acts accordingly, and the Holy Spirit does it through him.

There are several stories of Jesus healing people at a greater distance (Mt.8:5-13;Mt.15:21-28;Jn.4:43-54). Some have likened this to petitionary prayer but in each case Jesus declares healing rather than asks God for it. Whether Jesus is present physically or not 'the healing model of Jesus' still seems to fit. The authority of God the Father and the power of the Holy Spirit enable Jesus to heal the sick. Peter certainly saw Jesus' healing ministry in this way.

'You know what has happened throughout Judea, beginning in Galilee after the baptism that John preached - how God anointed Jesus of Nazareth with the Holy Spirit and power, and how he went around doing good and healing all who were under the power of the devil, because God was with him' (Acts 10:37,38).

THREE

The Healing Model of Jesus' Disciples

The impression we have formed from the New Testament is that Jesus did not heal people because he was God but because he was perfect man full of the Holy Spirit. The fact that Jesus' disciples were also able to heal the sick confirms this impression. If Jesus healed people simply because he was God, his disciples would not have been able to copy what he modelled, and thus follow in his footsteps. But they were and they did.

When Jesus had called the twelve together, he gave them *power* and *authority* to drive out all demons and to cure diseases, and he sent them out to preach the kingdom of God and to heal the sick (Lk.9:1,2).

The authority which comes from the Father and the power which comes from the Holy Spirit is now available to the disciples through Jesus. The healing model of Jesus' disciples looks something like this.

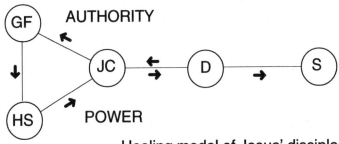

Healing model of Jesus' disciples

The disciple comes through Jesus to God the Father for the authority to heal the sick, and through Jesus to the Holy Spirit for the power to heal the sick. But, once both have been received, it is the disciple who heals the sick. Jesus says to them:- 'Heal the sick, raise the dead, cleanse those who have leprosy, drive out demons. Freely you have received, freely give' (Mt.10:8).

Just as Jesus prayed much to the Father and prayed specifically for Lazarus before he came to the tomb (Jn.11:41) so he taught the disciples to pray and go on praying. In Luke 11:1-13 he instructed them to ask and go on asking, to seek and go on seeking, to knock and go on knocking, and the object of their request is the Holy Spirit.

'If you then, though you are evil, know how to give good gifts to your children, how much more will your Father in heaven give the Holy Spirit to those who ask him!' (Lk.11:13).

In the previous two chapters Jesus himself gave power and authority to first the twelve and then the seventy-two to heal the sick. This teaching on prayer seems to be equipping the disciples for when Jesus is no longer present in the flesh. They are not instructed just to ask God to heal the sick. They ask God for the Holy Spirit who through Jesus will provide them with the authority and the power to heal the sick.

The difference between the Jesus model and the disciples' model is that Jesus did it in his own name but the disciples do it all, 'in Jesus' name.'

'Lord, even the demons submit to us in your name' (Lk.10:17).

Jesus gave them and us this promise:

'Anyone who has faith in me will do what I have been

24

doing. He will do even greater things than these, because I am going to the Father. And I will do whatever you ask in my name' (Jn.14:12,13).

In the next few verses Jesus links his going to the Father with the coming of the Holy Spirit.

'And I will ask the Father and He will give you another Counselor to be with you for ever – the Spirit of truth' (Jn.14:16,17).

So all Jesus' disciples, filled with the Holy Spirit, can do 'in his name' what Jesus had been doing. They can all heal the sick.

The endings of the gospels according to Matthew and Luke continue the themes of **authority** and **power**. Matthew records this:-

'Then the eleven disciples went to Galilee, to the mountain where Jesus had told them to go. When they saw him, they worshipped him; but some doubted. Then Jesus came to them and said, "All **authority** in heaven and on earth has been given to me. Therefore go and make disciples of all nations, baptising them in the name of the Father and of the Son and of the Holy Spirit, and teaching them to obey everything I have commanded you. And surely I am with you always, to the very end of the age"' (Mt.28:16-20).

Notice the emphasis here is upon **authority**. Notice also the command is to teach the new disciples 'to obey everything I have commanded you' (Mt.28:20). Authority and obedience go hand in hand. A Roman centurion has authority because he is 'under authority' (Mt.8:9). If he does what the Roman Empire tells him to do then the might of the Empire will back him up. If Jesus' disciples do what Jesus tells them to do then 'all authority in heaven and on earth' (Mt.28:18) will back them up. One of the things Jesus commanded his disciples to do, that they are required to teach new disciples to do, is to heal the sick (Mt.10:1,8; Lk.9:1,2;10:9).

Matthew highlights **authority** while Luke places more emphasis upon **power**.

'I am going to send you what my Father has promised; but stay in the city until you have been clothed with **power** from on high. When he had led them out to the vicinity of Bethany, he lifted up his hands and blessed them. While he was blessing them, he left them and was taken up into heaven. Then they worshipped him and returned to Jerusalem with great joy. And they stayed continually at the temple, praising God' (Lk.24:49-53).

Luke also repeats the stress on 'power' at the start of his second volume.

Jesus said to them: '...you will receive **power** when the Holy Spirit comes on you.... After he said this, he was taken up before their very eyes, and a cloud hid him from their sight' (Acts 1:8,9).

Authority and **power** are what Jesus gives to his disciples to enable them to do everything he had been doing.

After the Holy Spirit has been given to the believers in Acts chapter two we find the healing ministry of Jesus continues. Four things are worth noting about the early disciples who healed as Jesus healed.

A. **They are filled and go on being filled with the Holy Spirit**.

Peter receives power to heal the sick in Luke 9:1. After the resurrection, before the ascension, he receives the Holy Spirit again from Jesus in John 20:22. After the ascension in Acts 2:4 he is 'filled with the Holy Spirit.' In Acts 4:8 before the Sanhedrin Peter is 'filled with the Holy Spirit.' In Acts 4:31 at a prayer meeting he is once more 'filled with the Holy Spirit'.

Three times Luke writes that Stephen is a man 'full of the Holy Spirit' (Acts 6:3,6:5;7:55); once that he is 'a man full of God's grace and power, who did great wonders and miraculous signs among the people;' and once that he spoke by the Spirit (Acts 6:10).

Paul is filled with the Holy Spirit in Acts 9:17 and 'immediately' his sight is restored. In Acts 13:9 he is 'filled with the Holy Spirit' and this time gives blindness to Elymas. After persecution in Pisidian Antioch he is 'filled with joy and the Holy Spirit.' Not surprisingly he commands the Ephesians who have already received the Holy Spirit, (Eph.1:13) to 'be filled with the Spirit' (Eph.5:18). The Greek means 'go on being filled.'

B. **There is evidence of prayer in Acts but no use of 'the prayer model' to heal the sick**.

In chapter nine Peter is asked to raise Tabitha from the dead. 'Peter sent them all out of the room; then he got down on his knees and **prayed**' (9:40). But – after he has prayed – Peter then speaks the words of healing. 'Turning towards the dead woman, he said, "Tabitha, get up"' (9:40).

When Paul arrives in Malta he discovers from Publius, the chief official of the island, that his father is sick in bed, suffering from fever and dysentery. 'Paul went in to see him and, after **prayer**, placed his hands on him and healed him' (28:8).

In both cases there is prayer but God uses the one who prays to exercise faith, with a command or laying-on-of-hands.

Luke writes, 'God did extraordinary miracles **through Paul**' (19:11). The disciples in the Acts of the Apostles do not appear to have played much golf. They go to the sick people in Jesus' name and heal them.

C. **The believers in Acts are all familiar with God speaking to them directly, by His Spirit**.

Peter knows when Ananias and Sapphira have lied to the Holy Spirit (Ch.5), and is told by God to go to the Roman centurion, Cornelius (Ch.10).

'The Spirit told Philip, "Go to that chariot and stay near it"'(8:29).

Paul is told to go to Macedonia, (16:9), guided throughout his missionary journeys (18:9-11) and led safely by God to Rome (27: 23-25).

All three were used greatly by God to heal the sick (Acts 5:15,16;8:6,7;19:11,12).

D. **The disciples healed people 'in the name of Jesus'**.

'Then Peter said... "In the name of Jesus Christ of Nazareth, walk"' (Acts 3:6).

'Peter said to him, "Jesus Christ heals you"....'(Acts 9: 34).

...Paul became so troubled that he turned round and said to the spirit, "In the name of Jesus Christ I command you to come out of her!"' (Acts 16:18).

The early disciples are filled and go on being filled with the Holy Spirit. In Acts Chapter Four it happens during a prayer meeting. No-one uses the healing prayer model, but Peter (Acts 9:40) and Paul (28:8) are both recorded as praying before speaking, healing and using the laying-on-of-hands. The first believers are familiar with God speaking to them directly. When Paul is used to heal a man in Lystra he 'saw that he had faith to be healed'(Acts 14:8-10), and he eventually discerned, after 'many days' (Acts 16:18) that a girl in Philippi needed deliverance. They healed people 'in the name of Jesus,' which implies they did it with Jesus' authority.

Thus it can be argued that the same pattern appears to be emerging. The disciples pray to God, they are filled with the Holy Spirit, they discern God's will, and they are used by God to do the healing. This is a pattern we have found sometimes works today.

Prior to speaking at a meeting in Aldridge, where I'd never been before, I prayed and asked God to send His Holy Spirit upon me. As I sat for a moment to compose myself, a wave of heat came across my forehead, so I closed my eyes and asked God what was happening. The physical sensations of heat and power which indicated to me the presence of the Holy Spirit were accompanied by a 'knowing' in my mind that God was going to give me a 'word' for physical healing.

The word 'inter-ventricular' formed in my mind. I did not know what this meant, but looked it up in a dictionary and realised it was to do with the heart. As I gave out the 'word' at the meeting, Jan Coleman was in agony. Two or three times a week she suffered very painful palpitations due to a damaged left ventricle, and she was having one now. This is Jan's account of what occurred:

'Towards the end of the last song before the ministry began, the palpitations started and so did the chest pain, which became quite severe – legs were trembling and weakness spread throughout my body. No one else in the church knew that I was actually having an attack then, but a few friends knew of the problem. I slumped into the chair in the hope that no-one would notice what was happening to me; also because my physical strength seemed to desert me. When Peter gave the word 'inter-ventricular' it was as if God was calling me by name. I was upset that He had allowed this to happen in church, and I started to weep. Several people who knew I had this complaint reached towards me and said, "That's you Jan, go on." Although my desire was to hide – I didn't want to be exposed – I couldn't fight it and it was not with my own strength that I rose and struggled forward. I was really surprised when I found myself heading towards the front of the church.'

When people laid hands on Jan Coleman, power went right across her chest, and her heart seemed to stop beating. 'I'm dead', she thought, but eventually realised it was just the palpitations stopping. She hasn't had any since. [1]

I prayed, God filled me with His Holy Spirit and gave me a 'word'. As we obeyed God's 'word' and Jan received it, so in Jesus' name the power of the Holy Spirit came upon her and she was healed. The authority of the Father and the power of the Holy Spirit sometimes enable us to heal the sick in Jesus' name.

Notes

1. This account also appears in *The Hot Line*, op. cit. p56.

FOUR

Spiritual Gifts

As we move from the Gospels and the Acts of the Apostles to the Epistles, we find Paul's teaching on spiritual gifts fits well with what we have discovered so far. In 1Corinthians12 Paul informs us about spiritual gifts, listing nine different ones. Six of them are about hearing God. In 1Cor.12:2 Paul contrasts God with mute idols, and earlier in 1Cor.2:16 he has written, 'we have the mind of Christ.' These six gifts are all in keeping with the authority of God the Father. As with Jesus, and his early disciples, we too can hear the God who speaks.

The God Who Speaks (1Cor.12:8-10)
1. Message of wisdom
2. Message of knowledge
3   Prophecy
4   Distinguishing between spirits
5   Speaking in tongues
6   Interpretation of tongues

It is important we are not ignorant about the different gifts (1Cor.12:1) because they help us to identify when God is communicating with us. A man brought up in a jungle who moves into western civilisation needs to learn about telephones, televisions, hi-fi, letters, books, videos etc., so he can recognise and receive communications. But whether he receives a message by post, phone or fax is far less important than that he receives it. It is the God who speaks we seek, that we may come under His authority and do His will, rather than the gifts for themselves.

In my first book *The Hot Line* I wrote about the 'God who speaks' who lives inside every Christian. If we want to be used by God in healing the sick, it is important we learn how to receive spiritual gifts and to hear from God.[1]

The practical problem I often encounter is that Christians who have never received or used spiritual gifts do not know what it feels like. The fear of failure or rejection is also a common reality.

The natural mistake is to see spiritual gifts as abnormal, awe-inspiring, extra-terrestrial dollops. Consequently many people miss them when they come. The key is to recognise that the Holy Spirit lives inside us. He works with us, in us and through us.

So – a word of knowledge is just like an ordinary thought or impression. The other end of the dialogue. Shall I have carrots or peas for lunch? Carrots. Why is this person sick? She hasn't forgiven her brother. It feels no different. It is God inside us. It's just that when it happened to me in a counselling situation I asked if she had a brother, and it soon led to her telling me he'd molested her when younger. When she was cut off, forgave him and was healed - then I knew it was God speaking.

Everyone can speak in tongues, because we have a spirit. Disengage the mind, speak out and sounds will come. It is only inhibition which stops us. If you do it when playing golf it will probably come from self and be gibberish. If you go to a seance and try it, demons will affect the words and your personality. But try it in the middle of worship and praise to the God and Father of our Lord Jesus Christ, and sounds will come that God can inspire and take and use to His glory. It's that simple.

Worship is the trigger to spiritual gifts; followed by silence. Then back the hunches. If the God who speaks lives inside us, I expect He may want to communicate with us from time to time.

The remaining three gifts are connected with power. In 1 Cor.2:4, Paul wrote, 'My message and my preaching were... with a demonstration of the Spirit's power.' These three gifts are in keeping with the power of the Holy Spirit. As with Jesus and his disciples we can also receive and be filled with the God who comes, in power. 'Our God comes and will not be silent' (Ps.50:3).

The God Who Comes (1Cor.12:9,10)

7   Faith
8   Healing
9   Miracles

In my second book *Doing What Comes Supernaturally*, I wrote about the 'God who comes.' Many of us have found that by asking God to come and then waiting expectantly, His power often comes to us and upon us, enabling us to do what He wants us to do. [2]

In this exercise it is asking, expecting and waiting that counts. Again it is best following worship and with friends. We cannot receive the power to heal and know we can heal without someone else present, preferably someone who is not already perfectly whole. If power comes, especially in the hands, then we lay them gently on someone else's head and see what happens. With permission, of course.

During one cold winter's evening meeting I prayed for five different people called 'Mary.' On the first four occasions my hands heated up considerably as I prayed. One, at least, was completely healed of a physical complaint. When I came to the fifth, I was feeling full of faith and very pleased to pray for this lady, (with others present), who was needing prayer for a bladder condition. I placed my hands on her head and asked God to come to her. Nothing happened! My hands felt cold, reflecting the room temperature. 'Lord,' I said, 'nothing is happening. Why have you turned the power off?' Then I sensed Him telling me to lead her in a time of repentance, which I did, finding myself praying against fear and loneliness. At this moment my hands heated up like a kettle, becoming far hotter than they'd been all day. Mary said afterwards, 'How did you know? How did you know that my problem was fear and loneliness? No one knows that!'

The following week the bladder was as bad as ever but the fear and loneliness had gone. During our meeting, the power of the Lord was present for this lady to be healed emotionally, and I was guided how to minister by feeling God's power in my hands.[3]

When asking God to come, it is so often the silence and the waiting afterwards which is important. God is not usually in as much of a hurry as we are. Doing it in small groups with permission to fail is the learning place for receiving and using spiritual gifts.

When God the Father speaks to us about a particular

person and a particular condition, and the Holy Spirit comes in power, then we can expect to see the sick healed. I have not met anyone who regularly sees the sick healed in the name of Jesus who does not also regularly receive spiritual gifts from God.

Notes

1. Op.cit. *The Hot Line*
2. Op.cit. *Doing What Comes Supernaturally*
3. This account also appears in *The Hot Line* op.cit. p.117

FIVE

Wholeness

So far we have looked at healing from the point of view of those seeking to minister as Jesus ministered. There were times when sick people (who were healed) appeared to be quite passive in their response to Jesus. The man in John 5 had no faith, the man in Luke 5 was brought by his friends, the blind man in John 9 only became a believer after he was healed – and – there were three dead bodies (Lk.7:12;8:53; Jn.11:17). But there were other times when the right response to Jesus was also highlighted by the evangelists (Lk.7:5; 8:48;17:19;18:42).

When Peter healed the cripple at the temple gate, in the name of Jesus, the man asked for alms but received legs (Acts 3:1-10). In contrast, when Paul healed the cripple in Lystra the man himself 'had faith to be healed' (Acts 14:8-10). Sometimes the attitude to Jesus of those praying for the sick is the most important one, and sometimes it appears to be the response of those who are sick themselves. In this chapter we shall look at Christian healing from the sick person's point of view.

According to different doctors and psychiatrists I have heard at different times, as many as 70% - 90% of all illnesses in the West may be due to psychosomatic reasons. Often, when analysed, these come down to thinking, believing and living in the wrong kind of way. At the heart of much of it is a spiritual sickness which can only be put right by faith in Christ.

When people want to be healed they usually mean, 'I want to be as I was back there.' Like fixing the television when it breaks down. Replace the worn out valve and all will be well again. But if I became ill because of psychosomatic reasons, then being as I was back there will only mean I shall become sick again. Fix the symptoms and not the root, and I'll have to keep taking the tablets. Christian Healing is primarily about putting the whole person right, with the side effect of becoming physically better. This being the case, it is often helpful to share about Christian maturity and wholeness when assisting a person to receive Christ's healing.

According to Paul, human beings have a spirit, soul and body (1Thess.5:23). The soul is not easy to define from the Bible but many people find the classifications of emotions, mind and will to be helpful. Tom Marshall pictures it something like this:[1]

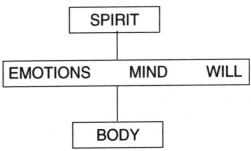

A human being as described by Paul

In the beginning, Adam and Eve were in perfect harmony with God, one another and the world. This meant their spirits, in union with God who is Spirit, controlled their emotions, mind, will and bodies. Made in the image of God, such a right relationship would mean a right image of God would be housed in their spirits, leading to a situation of complete wholeness. The whole picture looks like this:-

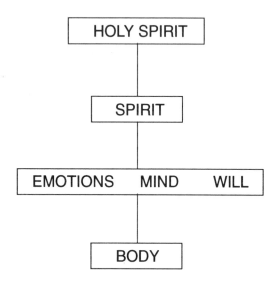

Adam & Eve before the fall

Unhappily, Adam and Eve sinned. The image of God was immediately distorted in their **spirits** and they became afraid of God. Their **emotions** dominated their behaviour as in fear and shame they ran away and hid. They now knew in their **minds** that they were naked so decided, (an act of **will**), to cover their **bodies**. Their sin led them to being driven from the garden and cut off from God. Their whole beings - spirits, emotions, minds, wills and bodies – were affected by sin. The Holy Spirit was no longer controlling their lives and behaviour. We can picture it like this:-

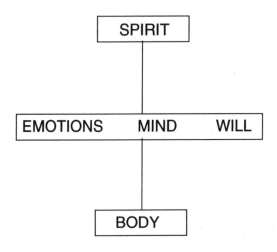

Adam & Eve after the fall

The Old Testament follows as a sad tale of how emotions, mind, will and body began to dominate people's lives instead of their Holy Spirit controlled spirits. This led to disharmony, dysfunctional relationships and dis-ease. Cain **felt** angry and murdered his brother (Gen.4:5-8). In Noah's time, 'every inclination of the thoughts (**mind**)... was only evil all the time'(Gen.6:5). The people tried by their own **will** power to build the tower of Babel to reach into the heavens (Gen.11:4), and fleshly appetites (**body**) ruled the city of Sodom and Gomorrah (Gen.19:1-29). Adam died (Gen.5:5).

By the time we reach the twentieth century, a new phenomenon has arisen: materialism. This is the philosophical doctrine behind humanism and communism, which has produced the secular society. According to this belief, human beings are only matter and have no spirit. The diagram of ourselves becomes much smaller:-

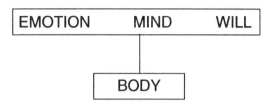

A human being as seen by the secular society

To digress for a moment into apologetics, this view seems to fly in the face of evidence. From the earliest records, mankind has always believed in life after death. (Note the Egyptian pyramids, the Red Indians' happy hunting ground and the Scandinavian Valhalla). Similarly, men and women desire to worship whether it is pop stars, sports stars or other idols. The secular society has its own 'gods'. Note also the cave paintings of early peoples. There is no evidence in the rest of the animal kingdom for belief in life after death (funeral rites) or worship. It could also be argued that such activities as art, music, poetry, dance etc., are inspired by the spirit which is in mankind. Malcolm Muggeridge, in 1974, summed it all up when he said that communism would inevitably fall one day because it was 'so boring'. Life without a 'spirit' let alone the 'Holy Spirit' is a colourless existence and this may explain the resurgence of interest in Eastern religions, 'new age' and occultism. But God has provided us with a better way.

God's only Son having been born, lived, died, risen and ascended into heaven now pours out the Holy Spirit on all believers. Through believing in what Christ has done for us on the cross, repenting of our sins and accepting him as saviour, we may be put right with God. We can be born again by the Holy Spirit. When this happens, the Holy Spirit gives new birth to our spirits (Jn.3:6) and it now becomes possible to be restored to wholeness in Christ. Paul describes what can happen in Romans 8.

The right **image** of God is restored to our spirit. '...By him we cry, "Abba, Father"'(Rom.8:15). The **Spirit** himself testifies with our **spirit** that we are God's children (8:16). We are now 'in Christ Jesus' (v1), which means having the 'Spirit of Christ' within us (v9). It becomes possible to live 'according to the Spirit' (v4) and be 'controlled... by the Spirit.'(v9). This leads to harmony and wholeness. Our **spirit** comes alive (v11), fear (**emotions**) is replaced by sonship (v15), and we are now free to choose (**will**) life rather than death (v13); a share in God's glory (v17) rather than sin (v12). This can be the beginning of healing and wholeness in the real world.

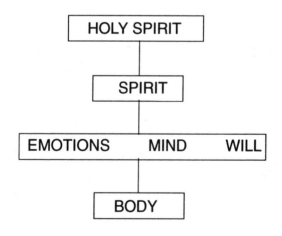

The Spirit-filled Christian

The Real World

Now let us see how this works in practice. A friend of mine was sexually abused as a child. We'll call her 'Marie'. By the time she was middle-aged her whole body was in constant pain through arthritis. The analysis goes something like this.

Marie's spirit is affected by the bad news coming up from the body, emotions, mind and will, rather than the good news coming down from the Holy Spirit. This leads to dis-harmony and dis-ease.

The body is abused and in pain. The emotions register major fear. The mind prays, 'Lord don't let Daddy do that to me again tonight.' But Daddy does. God must not care, not be powerful enough, or on Daddy's side. My will is crushed. I am a small child. I have no hope of escape.

The image of self is low. Maybe it is all my fault. The image of God is distorted. He does not love me. Maybe I am not worth loving. My emotions, mind, will and spirit feed negatives into my body, which reacts by becoming ill.

One day Marie meets some Christians. They accept her and love her as she is. Her spirit begins to be affected by the Holy Spirit in them. As they affirm Marie, so a little bit of self-esteem begins to grow in her will. Maybe there is hope.

The mind is a stumbling block. If God loves me, why did He let it all happen? Why did He not answer my prayers? Marie is helped to think through three stages.

1. The head of the Christian Church is an abused victim. Naked on a cross he suffers for the sins of the whole world. Marie's spirit has not met that image of God before. She studies it and meditates upon it.

2. How did she feel when father and uncle did things to her against her own will? Dominated? Trapped? In bondage?

God loves us and will never dominate us by taking away our free will, or the free will of father or uncle.

3. Now Jesus must be seen to be on our side. Forgiveness? Can Marie hate what happened to her? Oh yes! Jesus wants us to hate sin. He hated it too. Can Marie hate abuse for the rest of her life? Good. Jesus wants us to hate sin for the rest of our lives. Can we forgive those who sinned against us? 'As long as you are not asking me to say what happened to me was OK! As long as I can hate what happened to me for the rest of my life. Maybe I can forgive.' Jesus hates sin and loves sinners. That is fine.

Marie asked Jesus Christ into her life. His Spirit came on her spirit and began to build her up with his love. One day she went and forgave her mother. She always felt mother was the one who could have stopped it. When forgiveness was offered and received, the arthritis left.

Each morning, as soon as Marie woke up, she said out loud, 'I choose to forgive my mother today.' She did this for six months until the new way of thinking became part of her new nature. The arthritis did not return.[2]

So often wrong thinking, wrong beliefs, and wrong practices coming from bad experiences, lead us to inherit the rewards of the kingdom of darkness. When the Holy Spirit comes, he does so to bring in the kingdom of light – God's kingdom. When we begin to live in the light and walk in the light the darkness is often dispelled. Following the **whole** counsel of God is the path to **wholeness** in spirit, emotions, mind, will and body.

This is why healing sometimes takes a long time. This is why some people are healed in church on Sunday and ill again in the world on Wednesday. The aim of Christian healing is not just to restore us to what we were, but to renew us to become more like Jesus. The Christian counsellor will always be concerned with the symptoms and seek to help and alleviate these as quickly as possible, but there are very few short-cuts to Christian maturity. Thinking, believing and living in the right kind of way, controlled by the Holy Spirit, who opens up the scriptures to us and brings in the love of Christ through his body the church, is the most effective way to receive God's healing and wholeness. Sometimes, when God helps us to change the way we think and live, we are healed.

Notes

1. Tom Marshall *Free Indeed* (Sovereign World, Chichester 1975) p154.
2. The story of Marie is recorded in *Doing What Comes Supernaturally* op. cit. pp207 - 208.

SIX

The Cross

Sometimes when we are born again and become Christians we begin to feel physically better. We are saved by the blood of the Lamb. Sometimes when the Holy Spirit comes powerfully upon us we are healed. We can ask the Father to send the Holy Spirit because of what Jesus has done for us on the cross. Sometimes when we confess our sins we are healed (James 5:16). This is because sickness may be connected with sin and we can receive forgiveness through the cross (Lk.5:20,Jn.5:14). Sometimes when we receive forgiveness and affirmation from God, we can freely choose to forgive and affirm another, and find we are healed. This is due to the cross. We forgive because He first forgave us. Sometimes the Holy Spirit helps us to discern, and cast out a demon or two, and the person is healed. We can do this because Satan and all his army were defeated at the cross (Col.2:15). Sometimes as we stand in the presence of God we forget about ourselves, concentrate on Him and are healed. We can stand in the presence of God because Jesus has died for us on the cross. I have seen almost every good, Christian, spiritual activity lead someone to physical healing at different times, and all are linked in some way with the cross of Christ.

But nowhere can I find in the New Testament that physical healing is our covenant right because of the cross. What I have described are indirect links to the cross. Without Jesus' death they would not be possible, but physical healings are not automatic because of the cross. The New Testament does not say we can claim physical healing because of Good Friday. Some sicknesses that are directly connected to sin or demons can be healed by applying the cross to them in faith. But those which are not (e.g. Jn.9), and are due merely to the consequences of living in a fallen world, need the authority of God the Father and the power of the Holy Spirit through the name of Jesus before we can command a healing.

People have tried to claim healing directly linked to the cross on the basis of New Testament verses but this is not an easy or obvious interpretation of scripture. Two verses in particular may need comment.

'He himself bore our sins in his body on the tree, so that we might die to sins and live for righteousness; by his wounds you have been healed' (1Peter 2:24).

The context is forgiveness of sins - spiritual healing - the most important. Nowhere in the whole letter does Peter write about physical healing.

'This was to fulfill what was spoken through the prophet Isaiah: He took up our infirmities and carried our diseases' (Matthew 8:17).

This time the context very definitely is physical healing but there is no mention of the cross or Jesus' atonement. Jesus took away their sickness – a sign of the coming Messiah. The reference is used in Matthew, nineteen chapters before the cross. Some argue the cross works backwards and Jesus could heal because he knew he was going to die, but it is not what the New Testament says.

What the New Testament does say again and again is that in the power of the Holy Spirit, under the authority of God the Father, Jesus, the disciples and his other followers can heal the sick. Spiritual wholeness, which sometimes leads to physical healing and sometimes does not, can be received by walking in the Spirit, and engaging in good spiritual activities such as worship, Bible reading, fellowship, prayer, holiness and righteousness. Such opportunities are all made possible to us by God's grace and Jesus' sacrifice.

But the cross makes it possible for the healing work of Jesus to continue – not to be changed. Jesus did not heal people because of the cross. He healed people whenever his Father gave him authority, and the Holy Spirit gave him power. The cross means that we too can be called children of God and do what Jesus did, the way Jesus did it.

In 1988, I went with John Wimber to South Africa. From time to time he kept chuntering, "'would that my enemy would write a book.'" He had written a wonderful book called *Power Healing*, which was well received by the Christian public, but his critics had noticed there was no mention of the cross. He was greatly upset, because so much of his life and ministry has been centred on the cross. But he was absolutely right. Healing in the New Testament is always linked to the Holy Spirit and never directly to the cross.[1]

To believe that healing is mine as a covenant right because of the atonement is to deny **everything** the New Testament says about physical healing, and to claim something as true that the New Testament **never** says. It is a belief that has many problems.

1. **There are theological problems**. John Stott writes:
'Bearing the penalty of sin is readily intelligible, since sin's penalty is death and Christ dies our death in our place but what is the penalty of sickness? It has none. Sickness may

itself be a penalty for sin, but it is not itself a misdemeanour which attracts a penalty. So to speak of Christ 'atoning for' our sicknesses is to mix categories. It is not an intelligible notion.' [2]

2. **There are biblical problems**. If people were healed by claiming their covenant rights we would not need the Holy Spirit and we would not need spiritual gifts. Who needs the spiritual gift of healing if healing is already mine by right? Who needs to hear from God and who needs to discern when He comes in power? In fact, who needs God at all? If God put my healing in the bank at Calvary I can simply go and draw it out without bothering Him. The Bible suggests otherwise. The New Testament links healing to the coming of the Holy Spirit in power, and describes spiritual gifts as the keys to tapping into that power.

3. **There are assurance problems**. It is a doctrine which can lead me to doubt my own salvation. I am saved by believing in what Jesus did for me on the cross. If I am also healed by believing in what Jesus did for me on the cross, where does that leave my salvation if I am not healed? If I have not enough faith for healing, what makes me think I have enough for salvation? The logical conclusion is that every so-called Christian who wears spectacles, needs a hearing-aid, has a cold or dies of a disease is not saved.

4. **There are compassion problems**. I have heard people shouting at those in wheelchairs to have more faith. That is not healing, that is abuse. And who should have the faith anyway? In the New Testament it is often the one ministering or the friend or the relative who has the faith. And faith in what? My healing ministry? My reputation? My dodgy theology?

5. **There are historical problems.** It is a belief which totally denies the history of revivals. At times, during revival, such as Indonesia in the sixties, many people were healed. But - the same people who laid hands on people before the revival and after the revival, found that far fewer people were healed then than during the revival. Why? Because supernatural healing comes from God and a movement of His Holy Spirit. That's what the New Testament says and that's what the history of revivals demonstrates.

6. **There are practical problems**. It doesn't work and in particular it doesn't work in the West. Those who preach it see some healed, occasionally many, but never all of everything. They don't empty hospitals. The belief that healing from all sicknesses can be claimed as a covenant right for all Christians, for all times, has never been demonstrated.

So why do many Christians believe in healing as a covenant right? It is simply because in their own human minds they cannot accept God heals some and not others. This is a logical problem but it is not a theological one, nor a New Testament one. Interestingly, many who believe in 'healing as a covenant right', also claim to believe totally in the authority of scripture, and yet their way of operation is exactly the same as the liberal theologians. Liberals cannot accept that God heals some and not others, so they do not believe God heals anybody. Consequently, they throw out all the healings mentioned in the Bible. This is the danger of deciding with my limited and finite brain what God can and cannot do. From the same starting-point, (non-acceptance that God heals some and not others), 'liberal' theologians and 'healing as a covenant right' theologians end up at totally opposite ends of the spectrum, if indeed they are still on the same planet. I suggest, therefore, it is the starting-point which is the problem. It seems far better to me to accept God's revelation to us, even if we do not always understand it. If we do this, a more balanced and biblical view follows on naturally.

We rejoice to hear of Peter's deliverance from jail (Acts 12:3-10), but remember James had just been killed with the sword (Acts 12:2). We are thrilled to read how Paul raised Eutychus from the dead (Acts 20:9-12), and commiserate with Timothy who had tummy trouble and frequent illnesses (1Tim.5:23). We recognise it is the same God who brought Moses and Joshua out of Egypt (Exodus), and rescued Daniel from the mouth of the lions (Daniel 6); but with sadness of heart we read of Stephen's death by stoning (Acts 7) and the early Christian martyrs who were fed to the lions in Rome. We acknowledge that the words of Jesus are still very true today. '..there were many in Israel with leprosy in the time of Elisha the prophet, yet not one of them was cleansed - only Naaman the Syrian' (Lk.4:27). And we give thanks for modern Christians like Joni Eareckson Tada who has led more people to faith in Christ from her wheelchair than most of us who have two good legs. [3]

It is also worth noting that some non-Christians are healed by Christ. In the Gospels and Acts some people are healed first and then believe in Jesus (Jn.4:53;9:35-38; Acts 3:8,9:8:12;9:18;28:8-10). Today the same is true. Rather than being healed by believing in the cross and claiming their covenant rights, some are healed first by Christ then believe in the cross and then enter the New Covenant relationship with him.

Dr. Duncan Gee M.B.,Ch.B., was born with a squint. As 'Bog-eye' he endured much taunting at school. As an adult he could drive a car with one eye on the road and one on the rear-view mirror. Dr. Chris Moran, a consultant in our congregation, said he could not bear to look at Duncan eye to eye, even if it had been possible.

Unbeknown to Duncan, his wife Anne, also a doctor, was the first in the family to become a Christian. So, when one of his patients invited him to a Full Gospel Business Men's dinner to hear an American doctor speaking, there was prayerful encouragement at home. Duncan went.

The speaker went on for over two hours and then prayed for a man with back trouble. 'Look!' he said. 'One of your legs is shorter than the other.' After prayer, he announced, 'Now your legs are the same length.'

Dr. Gee's response was immediate. 'What a load of rubbish!' he thought. 'If you have back problems you get a bit of pelvic tilt, then a touch of muscle spasm and that makes one leg look shorter than the other.'

But, before Duncan could escape, the American invited everyone present to join hands while he prayed for them to be filled with the Holy Spirit. Our beloved physician was trapped and found himself taking part. Nothing happened.

Two days later Duncan went to church with his wife, because the children liked the Sunday School. He didn't know the American doctor was the guest speaker. After a shorter homily he invited people to come forward for healing prayer. Duncan didn't move but, sitting where he was, eyes closed, asked God to let him see straight.

Immediately, he felt a tremendous pull in his left eye. He went out to his car and had difficulty driving home. Dr.

Duncan Gee was seeing in three dimensions for the first time in his life. By the end of the week, the constant tugging in his eye made it sore and both eyes watered copiously but, little by little, the discomfort went away, leaving Duncan completely healed.

Then – Duncan believed in Jesus and what he had done for him on the cross – he committed his life to Jesus, and entered into a New Covenant relationship with him.

For a while, patients booked appointments with Dr. Gee just to see his new eyes. Many also noted his new life. Today he is a very committed member of Canford Parish Church.

The cross is indirectly linked to all Christian Healing because through it we can all 'know God from the least to the greatest'(Heb.8:7-13). It is this 'knowing' which enables us to discern when God wants to use us to heal the sick. The alternative approach, of trying to claim healing for every condition as a covenant right seems to me to be fraught with difficulties. I dare to suggest it is untenable, flying in the face of scripture and experience. I certainly want to retain the option of praying for non-Christians who have not, as yet, any covenant rights, as well as for Christians.

Sometimes when we pray for people they are healed. Sometimes when we lay hands on people they are healed. Sometimes when we gather in Jesus' name he releases spiritual gifts among us and people are healed. Sometimes when people's lifestyles are changed to be more like Christ they are healed. And sometimes healing is delayed a season until we meet Jesus face to face.

Notes

1. John Wimber, *Power Healing* (Hodder & Stoughton: London, 1986).

2. John Stott, *The Cross of Christ* (Inter-Varsity Press: Leicester, 1986), p245.

3. Joni Eareckson Tada writes about her tragic accident and how God helped her to come to terms with it in her book *Joni* (Pickering and Inglis: Glasgow, 1976).

SEVEN

'Name it and Claim it'

The Pentecostal church is the fastest growing church in the world at the moment. Throughout the twentieth century they have taught the rest of us that Jesus heals today, and have demonstrated it in their meetings. Some of their better known preachers often encourage everyone to name their sicknesses before God and to claim their healing from Him in Jesus' name. Regularly, especially in their larger meetings, some are healed. The Pentecostal church probably sees more healings per square metre than any other church.

Mark 11:22-24 is one of the Bible references they frequently use to justify what some people describe as their 'Name it and Claim it' theology.

'Have faith in God,' Jesus answered. 'I tell you the truth, if anyone says to this mountain, "Go, throw yourself into the sea," and does not doubt in his heart but believes that what he says will happen, it will be done for him. Therefore I tell you, whatever you ask for in prayer, believe that you have received it, and it will be yours' (Mark 11:22-24 see also Matt.21:21-22).

This is the quotation most likely to be interpreted, 'If I really believe I am going to have whatever I ask for, I will receive it.' Can Jesus' words therefore really mean that if I ask to win the National Lottery and believe I'm going to win it, I will?

These are the conditions for asking, to be found in some of the other verses of the New Testament: 'Ask, seek, knock' (Mt.7:7; Lk.11:9); 'in my name' (Jn.15:16); 'if you do what I command' (Jn.15:14-16); if 'we obey his commands and do what pleases him' (1 Jn.3:22); and 'if we ask anything according to his will' (1Jn.5:14-15). James 1:5-8 is similar to the Matthew reference, but James himself says (in 4:2,3) 'When you ask, you do not receive, because you ask with wrong motives....'

The key seems to be asking in Jesus' name, and what this means is spelt out in John 15:7,14-16: 'If you remain in me and my words remain in you... If you do what I command... Then the Father will give you whatever you ask in my name.' I think when all the Bible verses are looked at together, and Scripture is allowed to interpret Scripture, then the overwhelming evidence is that we will receive what we ask for only when our faith is 'in Christ', 'in his name', and 'according to his will'. This is why we need to recognise God's voice and obey His commands before we can begin to pray in faith. There is a distinct difference between faith in Christ and faith in our own minds; between the power of the Holy Spirit and the power of positive thinking.

If a friend says to me, 'I'll pick you up by the post box at 6 p.m. and give you a lift to church,' I exercise faith in my friend by going to stand beside the post box at 6 p.m. If no-one says they'll pick me up and I go and stand by the post box at 6 p.m. in the hope of a lift, then I'm stupid. The difference between faith in God and stupidity is sometimes very small, like building an ark on dry land (Gen.6:11-22). It all depends on hearing the voice of God, knowing the mind of Christ, or interpreting the scriptures correctly.

Why then do those who believe in a 'name it and claim it' theology and claim every healing, seem to get better results than others? Here are a few thoughts.

1. Our God is a healing God who loves to heal (Ps.103:3).

2. Health and wholeness are signs of God's Kingdom (Rev 21:4). In contrast sickness is what Satan desires (Job 2:7; John 10:10).

3. In Scripture, the moments when God chooses not to heal, such as with Job for a season, are in a minority. This is particularly true of the New Testament. From time to time, God appears to allow sickness. Paul writes, '..I left Trophimus sick in Miletus' (2Tim.4:20). If we compare this, and Timothy's illnesses (1Tim.5:23) with the number of times recorded in the New Testament when God does heal through Jesus, we get a true biblical perspective. God loves to heal.

On most occasions, scripture describes a healing God, and indeed implies that healing is a sign of the advancement of God's kingdom (Lk.10:9). It should not, then, be surprising if Pentecostals believe God wants to heal every disease all of the time when, in reality, God wants to heal most sicknesses most of the time. Nor is it surprising if they get better results than those who believe that God only wants to heal a few people some of the time.

But there are other considerations. Most of the dramatic Christian healings today occur in the third world. The Pentecostals in Britain are not seeing the large numbers of healings that the Pentecostals in South America, Africa and Asia are seeing. Assuming the reports and claims to be largely accurate, (and this is sometimes difficult to verify), the following points may also need to be borne in mind.

1. People's simple faith in Christ in the third world is not

easily affected negatively by the so-called, 'Western scientific world view.' According to the Bible, the real world, the spiritual world, is the unseen world (2Cor. 4:18). By and large the people of the third world find it easier to believe in the real world. When I travelled around Malawi it felt much more like the world of the New Testament to me than the secular world of inner city Birmingham. I also saw the most dramatic and instantaneous healings when we broke the 'curses' of the witch doctors. Naming the name of Jesus and having faith in him was certainly all that was needed in those cases.

2. Jesus had compassion on the needy (Mt.9:36;14:14; 15:32;20:34; Mk.1:41;6:34;8:2; Lk.15:20), and in a world with few hospitals and medicines he frequently met their needs. On the other hand, he consistently opposed those who sought signs and wonders (Mt.12:39; Lk.11:29, Jn 4:48) rather than himself; healings rather than the healer. These days it would be very difficult for miracles in the West not to attract sensational media coverage. Kurt Koch, writing about the revival in Indonesia, predicted it would die out once Mel Tari's book was published in America. And it was so.[1] If God grew a new leg for someone with millions watching on television, would Christianity remain by faith rather than by sight?

3. Although I have no extensive facts and figures to support this, my limited experience of places such as Africa is of children who are precious, loved, affirmed, and rarely abused by their own families. Inter-tribal warfare is sometimes horrendous but parental affirmation of each individual child is very strong. When I lived in Malawi with thirty clergy families for a short time, I never heard any adult shout at a

child and hardly ever heard a child cry. The children who make it into adulthood are often psychologically well-balanced and more trusting than some wealthy westerners. They more easily trust friends, preachers, pastors, and God. And perhaps, most importantly of all, this means the problems of sickness are not so much psychosomatic as lack of nutrition.

I suspect the main reasons the Pentecostals in this country see relatively few healings is that they often fail to grapple with the differences between Christian Healing in the West and in the third world. If people are sick due to lack of affirmation rather than nutrition, then making them feel even more guilty for their 'lack of faith' will not normally improve the situation. God's willingness to heal must always be balanced with the things we need to change in our lives in order to receive His healing.

The main difficulty I experience in the West is that we cannot 'name it and claim it' and expect good results if our lives are in a total mess. Marie would not have been healed from arthritis by people shouting at her. It needed the gentle affirming move of the Holy Spirit encouraging her to forgive her mother. And I suspect she would not have kept her healing if she had not known the root of it and how to deal with it.

But – if we do seek to put our lives right, if we do sense God is giving us authority and power to heal in any particular situation, then I really do believe we need to learn from the Pentecostals on how to 'name it and claim it' with conviction and perseverance. This is very much in keeping with those in the gospels who were praised by Jesus for their unwavering faith in him. I am convinced we do not see as many healings as God would like because we are too timid. Sometimes God speaks clearly and comes in power, but people are not healed because we do not hang in there long enough with determination. We often demonstrate our lack of faith with our lack of action.

When God told Elijah He would send fire, Elijah exercised faith by calling the people together, challenging the prophets of Baal, and pouring water on the sacrifice. When God told King Jehoshaphat they would not have to fight the men from Ammon, Moab and Mount Seir (2Chr. 20:14-17) he exercised faith by asking the unarmed Levites to sing and praise at the front of the army. When God told Jesus he would raise Lazarus, Jesus delayed two days, had the tomb opened, and spoke the words, 'Lazarus come out,' in front of all the people (Jn.11:43). Whenever God speaks, then demonstrating belief with the correct action is often what is required to produce the results.

Julia used to suffer from a bad back. On one occasion her family prayed for her, she went over in the Spirit at home and afterwards felt better. But some time later the back trouble returned and no amount of praying or ministering from others would shift it. Each time people prayed Julia felt blessed, loved and a little better for a short while, but not healed.

During my visit to South Africa in 1988 Christine, our lay reader, led the monthly Sunday healing service. As it progressed Julia, just like the woman in the Bible (Mt.9:21), kept saying to herself, 'If only I go forward I'm sure I will be healed.' Faith grew inside her to the point where she testified afterwards, 'I just knew I was going to be healed.'

This is the work of God. This is a 'word' from God. This is faith in God. It is not a person deciding for herself what to do and believing it – the initiative comes from God. Touching cloaks, handkerchiefs or shadows, receiving communion or anointing with oil is nothing to do with magic, special objects or special places. All these things stimulate faith because of their associations, which help people to believe and receive what God is doing. The children of Israel were not saved by blood on the doorposts. They were saved by God, but their obedience to Him by smearing the doorposts with blood was an act of faith which released God's saving and healing power.

Julia had several times received appropriate 'words' for others, and this seemed to be one for herself. At the healing service, Christine invited people to come forward to the communion rail for prayer, but nobody moved. This is the moment when it is necessary to begin exercising faith. It is amazing how hard British people find it to get out of their chairs or pews once in them. The battle raged inside, and eventually Julia rose slowly and eased her way forward. As she did so, others followed her example. She found it very painful kneeling and, even though she felt God's anointing as Mary and Alicia prayed, her back became no better, so they stopped. This is the test of faith: imagine kneeling, in agony, at a communion rail, with two ladies on the other side praying, sensing God wants to heal, but experiencing no improvement. This was particularly difficult for Julia as so many had tried before. But she stayed with it. "You need to lay hands on my back," said Julia. So Mary leaned over the rail and put her hand in the right place. As they commanded the pain to go in Jesus' name, Alicia felt something move, and Julia's back was healed.

Next morning, the pain was back just as before. Now

comes a bigger test of faith! 'Did God really say...?' (Gen.3:1). Because Julia was convinced God had spoken and was speaking, she continued to resist Satan and the pain in her back, and fought in prayer for a whole week. After that the pain left and did not return.[2]

When God speaks, when power comes on people as we pray for them, then, I believe we need to 'name it and claim it.' We believe God wants to heal; we believe the Holy Spirit is giving us the power, so in Jesus' name we command the sickness and pain to be gone, and we hang in there as long as we can and as long as it is not causing distress to the sick person. On one occasion Jesus needed two goes to heal a blind man (Mark 8:22-26). Surely, this fact should encourage us not to give up easily the first time we try.

Sometimes when God wants to heal, and the Holy Spirit provides the power, naming it and claiming it in Jesus' name will bring healing. Perhaps if Christians from different denominations could learn from one another, we might all see more Christian Healing taking place in the West.

Notes

1. Kurt Koch *The Revival in Indonesia*, (Kregel Publications: Grand Rapids Michigan, 1971). He writes about the effects of Mel Tari's book *Like a Mighty Wind* (Creation House, Inc., 1971) in his preface.
2. This story first appeared in *The Hot Line*, op.cit. p125.

EIGHT

The Method

When somebody we know and love or someone in our church is taken ill, we move very quickly from the realm of heavenly wisdom to earthly reality. What shall we do?

A. We pray.

We pray for them to be healed. We pray for wisdom to know how to pray. We pray with others. We ask God to come and show us how to pray and what to do. If two or three agree on how to pray, we pray in that particular way. We pray openly, honestly and offer ourselves to God to be used in any way He chooses. If we sense God wants us to minister to the sick person, we ask the leaders of the church if this is acceptable. If it seems good to us, the Holy Spirit, the leadership and the sick person, we make an appointment to meet together.

B. We counsel.

One simple question may help us to highlight if there is a root problem and begin the path of wholeness. 'What was happening in your life the moment the symptoms first appeared?'

The only difficulty with this question is getting an honest answer. Although doctors say that 70% to 90% of all illnesses in the West are due to psychosomatic causes, only 10% to

30% of British people will ever admit it. This is where much prayer beforehand and the need for spiritual gifts comes into its own. Here are four examples of how this approach has helped me in the past.

Person 1.

Q. What was going on in your life the moment the cancer first appeared?

A. That's easy. I was promoted at work. I didn't want it. Everyone said I was the right person. I couldn't cope with the stress, the extra pressure, the responsibility. It was too much for me.

Person 2.

Q. How long have you had pain in the right ear?

A. Since we had drums in church.[1]

Person 3.

Q. When did the pain in your back and side first appear?

A. When my sister died.[2]

Person 4.

Q. Do you think there is anything we need to do first before asking God to heal your stomach pain?

A. No. It's a chronic illness. I've had it for twenty years. We've already been through all that.[3]

We minister

Person 1. We cut her off from the pain and hurt of the promotion at work. She talked a lot, and wept quite a bit.

Having chosen to accept the job she needed to forgive herself as much as the others. The Spirit of God came powerfully on her and gave her peace.

Person 2. The drums arrived in an Anglican Church. Not everyone approved. Some expressed their negative feelings publicly and vociferously. The man with the pain in the right ear was the drummer. We asked God to show him what Jesus thought about drums in church. He smiled from ear to ear. Maybe Jesus did not think the same as some of the Anglicans.

Person 3. The sister who died was 88. The one who was left was 86. Both were lovely Christians. No regrets. No disagreements. No problems at all. Knew she'd gone to heaven. 'Wish I was with her'. Ah! To choose death rather than life is to invite sickness and pain. There needed to be repentance.

Person 4. We accepted what the very mature Christian lady said and moved straight on to the laying-on-of-hands.

The Laying-on-of-hands

We lay hands gently on the person, usually on the forehead or shoulder, invite God to come and then wait in silence.

Person 1. We dealt with the promotion and stress while seated, which took about an hour. After this we stood and asked God to come in healing power. I laid my hand on her forehead and her husband put his hand gently on the stomach area, where the cancer was situated. The Holy Spirit came and she shook all over. At this point she was a little embarrassed, not having experienced such manifestations before. We assured her it was fine, then we commanded the illness to go in Jesus' name. She recovered well for a year and found a stronger faith in Christ before going to be with him.

Person 2. When the drummer stopped smiling and opened his eyes, I asked him how the pain was in the right ear. 'Terrible,' he said. So I placed my hand on his ear. 'In the name of Jesus, pain be gone!' I commanded. And it did. Immediately. And never came back.

Person 3. When the bereaved lady chose life and said a prayer of repentance, we asked God to come on the trapped sciatic nerves and He did. We commanded the pain to go in the name of Jesus and it did. So we all sat down for tea, and the pain came back. 'I do miss her,' she said. From then on every time she chose life the pain left - but whenever she expressed a desire to be with her sister it came back. It took several weeks for the pain to go finally. It is not easy to let a loved one go after 86 years. In a strange kind of way, the physical pain helped her to do this and to go on living for Jesus. The lady knew when she'd let her sister go finally. She was healed.

Person 4. On three consecutive days we prayed for the lady with pain in the stomach. On the first two days nothing happened. She thanked us for trying. We had one more go on the third day. I asked the Holy Spirit to come and show us what to do. Within a few minutes the lady said there were two people she needed to forgive. She forgave them. I placed my hand gently on her forehead and a lady colleague put hers on the stomach area. Once more we asked God to come. He came in power and the pain left. Several days later, the pain returned, so she re-visited the hospital. They had been trying to treat her for twenty years, without success. She spoke about what had happened when we prayed with her, so they took another X-ray. The medical staff were amazed.

The curvature of the spine, which we did not know about, had gone. The spine was now straight. Following further tests, they found that the spinal problem had masked an intestinal disorder, which was now correctable with surgery.

When the root of a problem is addressed, the coming of the Holy Spirit, and the commanding of an illness to go, is often quite dramatic and effective.

We encourage Christian maturity

When the spirit, will, mind and emotions have been subject to years of darkness, this will often be expressed in the body. The purpose of pain is to inform us that something is wrong. But having hated myself and the world, and having never trusted any human being, let alone God, for thirty, forty or fifty years, attaining wholeness and maturity is often a process - a journey rather than an instant solution. We need the Scriptures, especially the New Testament, to tell us about the true character of God and to guide us in right conduct. Both are best seen in Jesus. We need each other for support and encouragement, especially when pain after pain comes to the surface. We need a life of prayer to keep letting the Holy Spirit take more and more control over our spirits. We need a worshipping community to regularly lift our eyes from self, and to concentrate on God, who is our source of hope and joy and health.

When someone has been healed there are frequently new ways to think and to live if the person is to stay healed. Knowing the root of the problem always helps the person to know what to work on if the pain returns, as we saw with the bereaved lady. Christian healing is a path. Christ, the healer, is the prize.

What if I am not healed?

Whenever I talk about Christian Healing to a church that has never tried the laying-on-of-hands, they always ask, 'What if the sick person is not healed?'

When someone is first told they have a serious illness they are normally open to every kind of Christian ministry, for a while. We can try our best prayers, look for root causes, ask for spiritual gifts and command everything to be restored, renewed and revived. Sadly, there are times when nothing works. But – if we give time, love and sensitivity to people, lay hands on them gently and ask God to come, I cannot help feeling their spirits ought to improve even if their bodies do not. This is why 'wholeness' is sometimes a better word than 'healing'.

When I showed Sue what I had written about her and the liver transplant in Chapter One, she immediately reminded me of the healing from past hurts and emotional trauma which she had received from God while in hospital. I had inadvertently left it out. This inner healing certainly helped her to battle on through major surgery, tissue rejection, and the severe side-effects of the medication.

Time and time again, seriously ill people say to me, 'I don't feel any better, but do please come and pray with me again tomorrow.' On investigation, I find they are not usually saying, 'Maybe it will work better tomorrow,' but rather, 'I want more of the same.' In other words, 'My spirit enjoyed that. I feel loved and accepted and at peace.' Sometimes, of course, the laying-on-of-hands helps people to prepare for death.

With sensitivity, it is often right for Christian friends to pray, to offer the laying-on-of-hands (with the church leaders' permission), to counsel about possible root causes and, if God's authority and the Holy Spirit's power seem to come, to command healing in Jesus' name. In other words, at the start, we throw everything we've got into helping the person to be healed. I also encourage a seriously ill person to do everything the medical profession advises at the same time. This is never 'either- or', because God has also given us the natural world, our minds, years of experience, and common sense. 'Alternative medicines', which may have other spiritualities behind them, can be very dangerous, but physical illnesses approached physically are very much in keeping with what God has ordained. It is no different from drinking when thirsty or resting when tired. But having thrown everything into healing, the leaders of the church also need to keep an eye on progress, and to be aware of the dangers of trying to minister beyond the anointing.

If we are to become communities of healing and wholeness, we may need to be particularly aware of the different situations which can arise and need to be addressed. The following three activities are often overlooked by churches which have a 'healing ministry' but they may also bring degrees of healing.

i). SILENCING JOB'S COMFORTERS

Job was ill. The Bible tells us Satan caused it but God allowed it. There were no root problems or sins that needed attention. It was just the permissive will of God (Job 1 & 2). Job was completely innocent. Job's friends thought otherwise. They were obviously amateur theologians. If Job was ill, it must be due to sin. He should repent, and then maybe God would forgive him and heal him. They made the whole situation far worse. At a time when Job needed his friends, his friends became his enemies.

Jesus also ran into a similar situation. He encountered a blind man. His disciples asked him, 'Who sinned, this man or his parents, that he was born blind?' 'Neither this man nor his parents sinned,' said Jesus' (Jn.9:1-3).

It is easy for well-meaning Christian friends to become Job's comforters. One of the finest books I have ever read on Christian Healing is by Francis MacNutt.[4] He gives eleven common reasons why people may not be healed: reasons which may need some attention from the sick person. I can remember very well a friend of mine being disabled, and every day a different Christian knocked at the door, to accuse him or his wife with one or other of those eleven reasons. Sadly, he wasn't healed, and they separated. Pastors sometimes need to protect their flocks from well-meaning Job's comforters.

ii). **WELCOMING THE DISABLED**

Can you imagine sitting in your wheelchair while the preacher gives the weekly invitation for those with faith to be healed to come forward? It was not too bad for the first fifty-two weeks but, now you are well into your second year at the church, it is no longer a comfortable place to be. You already feel a burden. Big people have to be found every week to lift you up the steps as there is no ramp. You desperately want to go to the loo, but the chair won't fit in. You did go before you came out but you have to arrive earlier than the others for the long service, to make sure of a car-parking space.

Your church has the reputation of being a healing church

but sometimes it makes you sick. Perhaps the non-charismatic church down the road with better facilities and no pointing fingers might make you feel more whole. After all, your mind and spirit are not crippled and you do want to contribute.

A healing church will always make the disabled feel welcome, allow for it in their budget, and give opportunity for mind and spirit to be exercised.

iii). CARING FOR THE CARERS

People are living longer. At the beginning of the twentieth century, life-expectancy for a man was forty, and for a woman forty-five. With the advances made in modern medicine, people today often survive major accidents, but sometimes with serious resultant disabilities. Others are enabled to live longer with serious illnesses. The community is now, more than ever, required to provide constant care for such people. Loved ones do what they can. They want to, they ought to, and sometimes they've got to.

The carers are in our churches. Do they know they are loved? That God notices them and appreciates them? They can't often be at our mid-week meetings. They can't sit on committees. Frequently, they do not have much money to put in the plate. They can't put the chairs out for the services or come on the parish weekend or....

Does our healing church care for the carers? They can sometimes receive healing simply through offers of spouse- or Granny-sitting.

Sometimes when we pray for people they are healed. Sometimes when we lay hands on people they are healed. Sometimes when we gather in Jesus' name he releases spiritual gifts among us and people are healed. Sometimes when people's lifestyles are changed to be more like Christ, they are healed. Sometimes, when God gives a word and the Holy Spirit provides the power, naming it and claiming it in Jesus' name will bring healing. And sometimes God calls us to feed the hungry, give water to the thirsty, shelter for the homeless, land for the travellers, clothing for the naked, visits to those in prison and compassionate care to those who are sick, disabled or elderly (Mt.25:35,36).

'There is a time for everything, and a season for every activity under heaven' (Ecclesiastes 3:1).

We ask God for the wisdom and love to discern the season.

Notes

1. The story of the drummer was first published in *The Hot Line*, op. cit. p118.
2. A fuller account of this healing appears in *Doing What Comes Supernaturally* op.cit. p211.
3. This story is also recorded in *The Hot Line*, op.cit p113.
4. Francis MacNutt, *Healing* (Ave Maria Press:Indiana, USA, 1974).